My Business
Is
My Brand

Dharmesh Gajjar

DEDICATION

Word is so bigger, many among the world people have rights to do something best as brand image, this book is written for those people who are looking to expand their business on next level with developing their brand image with their business portfolio

In this book, contents are covered point to point with details descriptions the exact role of owner, employees & workers to reach your business next level with guidelines of by law of a business organizations.

This Book will help those one, who are looking to start their carrier as a business man or entrepreneur, those who are running their business which are stable or not getting better result, those who are old organizations but facing problems for their brand image.

CONTENTS

ACKNOWLEDGMENTS

I acknowledge those , who had taken my training, most of people or learner in training, asked me , having such wide and descriptive knowledge, you may have to write book, so we can read it and understand the methodology, so special thanks to them who encourage me to write this books. Also, I dedicate this book for learner who are looking forward their business growth.

CHAPTER: 1

WHAT WILL BE MY BUSINESS?

One day, when I was watching India's Cricket Match, I show the world-famous Cricket Player Sir Sachin Tendulkar, his Brand Name is Master Blaster, which indicate the Greatest Cricketer of world. At that time, I thought, is it not possible to make a brand of my name which directly indicate brand of my business (A Good Businessman). This thought inspired and motivated me to write a book that how an entrepreneur or a businessman make his/ her brand in their respective business portfolio. To reach this level to write a book, I decided, first to became a brand businessman, they have to look after the role of a businessman's problems and solutions.

Author, Mr. Gajjar has written many ways for successful businessman role and characteristics. Before entering in to any kind of Business as a businessman and entrepreneurship. Below points are most necessary.

As we know, when we are in to planning to get some things, we are trying and trying to get it. Because it is our moto or a goal. Same as, if I can say for doing any business or starting a business, it may be small or big, the businessowner have to be ready to work 24 hours of his total day time. Because, we have vision, goal, direction, destinations to reach on that level. We have to build such a stamina, enthusiasm or passion. If we don't have these three, we will be lazy and one day our business will be destroying or collapse.

"UNTIL UNLESS YOU ARE NOT CLEAR YOURSELF, YOU CAN'T START BUSINESS."

This is most important factor; you have to ask yourself. Because until unless you are not clear yourself, you can't start business. Not only asking this question is important, there are several questions which required respective answer. I can suggest you must have appropriate answers of several other questions. Which is most important factor to finally ask yourself "Should I be capable to start my own business?

Because some questions are those, which make you confused and demotivate, so first need to evaluate those other question. That will build your confidence and strength to decide to start your own business or run business.

We know. We have two type of mind conscious and unconscious. Some information is going in mind and which create ideas and innovations. But if you think to start business, is your first decision, which may be discontinue because of some several questions, so the decisions are in pending stage. First ask our self the bunch of questions to start business, which, we must have to solve, means, we have proper positive answers for that, then and then we can think about to the possible ways to start our business.

Few Question are as below?

> How much investments required to start business?
> How long it will take time to start?
> I have limited finance? in this limitation, will my business run well?
> Shall I start business this time? or have to wait for few years to start?
> In limited finance, can I go for other business or not?
> Shall I get success or not?
> After starting business, how much time required to get settle?
> Can my business run or close?

There are many more questions remains, which we have to understand and learn, there are some calculations,

"WHY NOT WE CAN MAKE OUR NAME WORLDWIDE BRAND IMAGE WITH OUR BUSINESS PRODUCTS NAME OR PRODUCT BRAND NAME"

It seems very interesting and confusing part of selections of our business and strategies. As an owner or entrepreneur, you must have an idea in your mind, what will be my own business after 5 years? Different technique to run my business? Planning and designing formats of our business. It will guide us the possible ways to start or execution of our business.

In the year 1999, when I was around age of 20, I was

traveling alone from Surat to Nadiad by bus, it was day time. I was listening the songs on Walkman stereo player. I was watching outside, noticed many industries, many people were working, some pickup trucks were standing outside the industries premises.

I was age of 20, questions raised in my mind, we have family members of 4 to 8 peoples, living together, run the family and facing so many problems. These industries have more 20 to 1000 peoples, why don't they have a problem? How these industries run? Any specific reason? So many questions were there in my mind. Same way every business man are thinking, but how to run is most important question?

"THE MAXIMUM BUSINESS OWNERS ARE NOT SCRUTINIZE THEMSELVES TO MEET THEIR REQUIRED GOALS."

I have personally experience of scrutinized a growth graph & relation of company owner to client and end-user of their products. I have seen, if the company owner is highly qualified, systematic organize ethics and systematic ways of working environments, then the business can become a biggest brand. Doing business is in such a way that, the whole world or your respective industries peoples will know you by your business name as a brand.

"THIS IS THE COMPNAY NAME AND THIS IS HIS OWNER"

Mr. Steve Jobs himself a brand name identify of an apple phone. Mr. Bill Gates himself known a brand image of Microsoft, because they have had made their company or a business in such a way that, every end uses have in their mind that Apple phone means Mr. Steve Jobs & Microsoft Intel Processor means Mr. Bill Gates.

Accordingly, to above examples. Why not we can make our name worldwide brand image with our business products name or product brand name? Question is interesting. it motivating us, but to be frank, yes, it can be possible.

To make this possible, we have to make some commitments and design some systems for our organization. If it is not possible to make this, but it seems very easy, because an owner can invest their money for factory, machineries, raw material, employees and workers, finally the outcome is a return of invested money, which is profit and business growth.

In addition, the owner must have to increase his business in profit making. This is only happening, when an owner or partners are design himself or change habits like Attitude, Responsibility among the Organization, simple meaning is to organize the business, same way to organize yourself.

Owner must be free from all activities of an organization, so they can think more and more to develop new era, innovations, expansion of business in next level for higher in profitable to create a valuable brand image. If owner is free, they have lots of many innovative ideas are there in their mind. Which force them for expansion and developments of their business.

To became a free from organization (business), first of all owner have to organize himself and then organize their business set up, like – Team, work, product details, systems and many more. This is the only techniques in which your business run very smooth. Systematics, tension free and stream line goal oriented.

"THINK BEFORE DO ANY THING WHO ARE YOU? WHICH WILL GUIDE YOU HOW TO PERFORM?"

Accordingly, above line, who are you is the most important for doing any kind of business. Can you do this? Can you organize your business properly? Can you handle all ups and down situation? So many questions are there, we have to think in details before design any plan, simultaneously, we have to set our mind accordingly set a plan for our business. So, all respective settled plan and thoughts will guide us how to perform easily, when will we have some sort of issue in business.

Every person (Entrepreneur of owner) must have to set their mind in their expertise era. Accordingly, their business goals are well-set. They understand that, their business is their brand. But maximums owners are not working as par to build up their brand and their business. There are some specific reasons, in which, the maximum business owners are not scrutinize themselves to meet their required goals.

Whenever, we are planning to set up a business. We must have to appoint (hire) an employee, who can work over in the business day to day. We are giving them an opportunity to show their talents, expertise knowledges, to complete the given work on time frame. To hire this type of employees with their expertise knowledge and talent. This make your organization is well organize and proper formats.

Above paragraphs, as you are planning to set up a business, the first question is, if you are looking a brand image or bigger picture of your company in your industries segment, you need to change yourself, change your strategies, change your ideas in such a way, that you have to became a creative, enthusiastic, motivation, and many more, this will build yourself a strategic personality to work on your business era.

"CONVERT YOUR MAXIMUM PROFITABILITY AND WORKABILITY AS WELL AS AN EFFICIENCY

THROUGHOUT THE BUSINESS ORGANIZATION."

Accordingly, other can follow and work as same as your ways. Because of above changes in yourself, it pays major role in your workplace. At the end, it will convert in your maximum profitability and workability as well as an efficiency throughout the business organization.

In year of 2007, I was working in one of the industries as export manager. That time I was engaged with my beautiful wife. She and her family knew that, I'm working in on of good Company, after 3 months of engagements, I decided to leave company and start my own business. At that time, I contacted one of company based Middle East (UAE), they gave me product of copper, which they want to place order, they share me the price, specification and other terms and conditions. They placed order of same price as a same they placed order to other suppliers.

"WE ARE GIVING THEM AN OPPORTUNITY TO SHOW THEIR TALENTS, EXPERTISE KNOWLEDGES, TO COMPLETE THE GIVEN WORK ON TIME FRAME."

My bad luck was that, I don't have idea from where, I can get the same material. Client gave me advance, that was golden opportunity to start my business, I was confused without knowledge, how can I supply material? A big Challenge was there.

I decided, let's try, may be some output I can get. I took Rs 15000 /- and checkbooks, went out of my city with single wearied cloths, after 12 days, I returned beck to my home with required material for exports. Visited Many cities like Ahmedabad, Rajkot, Bhavnager, surat, Mumbai, Pune & finally Nasik. I got that material from Nasik. I was earned 100 % Profit on that material.

I would like to share the important things, 12 days a single cloth, stayed at station, fully day eat only tea, bread and water, a dangerous 12 days passed, traveling here and there in day and night. If, I decided to not interested to go out to do all such struggle, then I will not earn 100 % of profit, or can't get experience to learn or develop my creativity.

This is clearly mention, that we have to forget the day and night, whenever we will have a work to short out as soon as possible, just keep it up till the work completed. There will be biggest happiness and achievement we get, because finally, we will have good amount of money in return. This kind of struggle and learning experiences, will guide us to tackle any kind of situation in our future business life.

Life is very big, when we will have an opportunity, we never have to wait, all doors are open, try to move maximum door. *"This will create your image as a brand"*. Who you are and what you do?

""" LIFE IS A BRANCH OF TREE, WE ARE JUST WALKING ON IT. WHEN WE PUT OUR LEG BESIDE THE RAW, WE FALL DOWN AT BOTTOM OF THE TREE""""

In above paragraph, you can observe, that I had left my ego, and try to achieve the goal. When I got the order, I thought it was not possible, but I tried and I grebe it, it was because of thinking with positive mind and set a goal to grab that opportunity. Yes, I grabbed, it was just for 100 % profit margin. Then after, whenever get orders, I earn 100 % margin. My business and my earning started smoothly.

To build up a successful Brand of your business, every

person or entrepreneurs must have to look forward their destiny, they must have aim to achieve their goal and path. But how to reach there?

You have to leave your ego, times durations, rejected, ridiculed, forget Sundays, working more than 12 hours, you must have to be in discipline & long-life earners. Always we get business opportunities, we have some skills to implement, if we think, not interested, you will be loss the business and learning experiences.

This was my first experience, I learned a lot, if we want to make your business as a profitable margin, we have to know how strong we are? the world is so big, we can earn more moneys in our business. We try to identify our self, short out our SWOT- S- Strength W- Weakness, O – Opportunity T- Threats.

Business is like a branch of tree- We have to walk over it, because our aim is to expand and develop our business. We have to up our graphs from one level to another level. We have to walk systematically and organize way with proper guidelines and positive manner. In above paragraph, I have had a confirm order, I tried to grebe it in systematically ways without thinking negative, just try and try, because I have planned to grow business and earn money, 12 days passed in unbelievable situation but finally I eat fruits.

"WE HAVE TO UP OUR GRAPHS FROM ONE LEVEL TO ANOTHER LEVEL. WE HAVE TO WALK SYSTEMATICALLY AND ORGANIZE WAY WITH PROPER GUIDELINES AND POSITIVE MANNER"

If, my internal thoughts are week, thinking negative, even something goes different directions, it means I can divert my walking steps on other side of raw, there may be possibilities, chances for fall down or return beck to initial stage, like (snack and ladder Game), and repeat the steps again and again. This is indicating the simple meaning, the businessman's goal, targets, ambition and enthusiasm are specified, simplified and time oriented.

If we think, doing business is very simple, but to maintain, is very difficult like customers. We do marketing for getting customer for our business, but it is very difficult that customer will place orders repetitively, the only reason is, we can't maintain customer properly, due to this, our business not grow well.

Same thing, we have to design our business model, first have to maintain our business as organize structure, we all know what business we are doing, and what type or kind of business we are looking to do?

"TO START THER IS NO NEED TOMORROW SUN RISE. WE HAVE ONLY NEED A NEW MIND SET TO SUN RISE ""

You are business owner, to run your business, there are some segments, where you have to focus, you have to set a people over there, who can work for grow your organization, that will make you free from doing work for your company. It means you may think more and more to develop and expand your business. You can make new time schedule to make you busy with attending meeting, conference, social life and family. That will increase and expand your business, you have to take new innovative ideas from other sectors to grow your company next level.

You as an owner, have to spend more and more time to think for yourself, your family, your business and your employees also. Which means you are leading yourself; you lead your business, employees for growth, internal & external developments. You have to follow the pirate formulas for your organization. You have to take and provide the training and developments to your organization.

Your soft skill nature is more help full for your employees to understand you and your organization in details, because you are their soft skill trainer, you must have co-ordination with your employees as a good teacher and student. We know the line- TICK TAK. Its means, if you are owner and teach well to your employees, you obey the system of your business, simultaneously your employees can follow and obey the systems, which you design or form, in result, you develop yourself and your organization, which grow up next level.

Remark: To better understand, we all have to determine our SWOT, Who I am? Check all the parameter in which, we can hold our attention. **"EXPERIENCE MAKE MAN PERFECT"** is the slogan, but we have to take participate in such an experience, so that we get 100 % Confidence in second time work. Which will give us better result to grow business.

Eg- I want to publish a book, I have written but don't have idea, how to publish and how much I can success, (it's difficult to do). Giving higher effort to search the book publisher, the book is published.

2nd time when I have to publish book, it's been very easy, we have 100 % confidence form every point of view. We learn among this experience and we share others also, who required knowledge.

CHAPTER: 2

WHAT SHOULD BE I AMFOR MY BUSINESS?

Everyone on this universe want to know, how to present ourselves in society, family, friends or in business industries segments. This is only happened, when we are trying to change our self, its means, we have to change attitude, behaviors, hobbits and many more, which is directly affect our image. It's clear that, sometime goal-oriented work or to achieve something, we have to became a selfish.

When, I was studying my master's in foreign trade. Staying in Collage Hostel. Final exam is coming next month, I had not prepared the subjects well, because of somehow busy in other work. So, I had 1-month time for exam. There were six subjects, I have to study in sort period. So, I decided to crack this exam with good scores of percentages.

To get a big score, I decided to make a plan and schedule like what time to study? What time to sleep? To whom to meet or to whom to ignore? etc. I totally change my attitude and behavior among other friends, I started giving concentrate on my study only.

Sometime my friends or my roommate said: Dear, let's go for have tea or snacks.

I said: sorry, you may go, I can't come.

They asked me again and again, - I started refusing, anger and said don't talk, let me do my study first. I started ignoring my friends. I had given notice to my roommate, don't make any kind of noise in the room, because I am studying here.

Due to above changes in my nature, attitude, behavior. I concentrated 100 % attention on my study because my target was to get good percentage in the exam.

Accordingly, above change in our behavior in our business profession, it will give us a better result to make profitable business long lasting.

"" IT IS NOT IMPORTANT HOW TELLENTED YOU ARE?? YOUR HIGHER EFFORT WILL ALWAYS HELPFUL TO BECAME A MORE SUCCESSFUL ""

I know, how talented I was to achieve good score in exam, I have not given any importance in any other work. I just paid attention and higher effort on my study with selfish nature to capture good exam scores, which made me success in academic.

Remark: Sometimes, we need to be serious and selfish, for the prototype targets, we have to achieve in our business or in life. To set a mind in such a way that, we can only focus on the target or work, we have to perform best possible and have to ignore unnecessary and un required things. Targeted work towards targeted path will gives return of success.

Simply to say, doing business, keep focus 100 Percent on your business work, when you are into business premises (business hours). Ignore all unnecessary disturbing things, which waste your time, 8 to 10 hours on business time, 100 % percent effort will increase your profitability, workability and efficiency of doing work. It also helpful to achieve big targets in short span, because you are habited to doing such thing.

Sometime, when we are running our business, we have teams, everyone wants to present themselves, who they are- (specially for owner, entrepreneur or employees who are leading the work). Main factor is our attitude. In our business workplace, our attitude creates our image, vice versa our Image create the image of our business organizations.

One Company had a big order. They had planned and taken in to production. They have defined the delivery date which was very fast. All workers & teams of company were doing their work. The last day of Productions, same day, at evening time they have to dispatch material, accordingly to contract of Purchase order, if company do late in delivery, big amount was deducted as a penalty (Late Delivery Penalty). So, the deadline came, last day at evening 7.00 p.m. they have to dispatch material.

Last day of Dispatch, the Productions was cut to cut, (going on as per schedule). The director came in factory before the time of office time. He called urgent meeting with all managements staff, to inform, today is our lest day, we all have to ready and dispatch material, so don't waste time, do focus on the work, we have onlt today.

After meeting, Director of company went to his office, sat on his chair and started watching CCTV in Tv. He notices all productions are going well. He felt himself happy and relax. He kept on CCTV, every 10 minutes, he noticed the productions, packing and other activities.

12-30 p.m. to 1.30 p.m. was the lunch time. He was planning to take lunch, before taking lunch, he thought, for my satisfaction let's check the cctv. He moved his eyes toward the TV, he noticed, all production teams, factory manager and operation management team were standing near production machineries, discussing to each other's about some issues over there.

12.30 p.m. to 1.15 p.m., director of company was continuously watching, he didn't take his lunch, he was thinking something goes wrong in productions, because during lunch time, all workers and teams were standing there, trying to sort out the problems, but not get result yet. They were trying and trying to resolve the issue.

In means time, Factory Manager and Operational Management team came to director's cabin for report the problem issue, they had in production. They sat front of director,

Drinking little water and said: Sir, we are having some technical problems in production.

Director Replied: yes, I am watching you all on CCTV since last 45 minutes, I thought there may be some issue in productions, but please wait, let me do on phone call.

Director call his Personal assistant:

Assistant: Hello Sir,

Director: Immediate Arrange a dining hall for 25 peoples

to lunch together,

Assistant: Yes, Sure, with in 10 minute it will be ready.

Director said to Factory manager: Let's take a lunch together now, then we will discuss the matter in details.

Both factory manager, and operational manager discussing each other, We have big problem in production but our director first insists us for taking lunch, He know, we have had and he also not taken lunch. He is taking care of us.

All went to dining hall for taking lunch together. Around 20-minute time spent for lunch, all employees were in tension. How can we make dispatch because of technical problems, they all are watching director face? His face was smiling and polite? He was talking with others freely- like nothing is happen.

After finishing lunch, Director said: Please share me the problem?

Factory Manager: Sir, we are trying to produce material but can't produce because of some machine technical issue. Our technician, electrical people tried their level best almost more than 1 hour, we are unsuccess to restart the machine. We are running delay in productions and dispatch.

Director Smiling, and said: That's great. It means, we are failure to restart the machine for further production. This is our failure, Lets enjoy, let's go to production unit and short out the troubleshoot to start again.

all 25 employees are reading director face and expression. He was smiling politely among other employees, all employees knew, if we are late in today's dispatch, we have a penalty clause in purchase order, which may be biggest loss for our company.

From all employees, one employee said: Sir, why are you

not serious ? this is big issue, we tried our level best to sort out the problem, but you said lets enjoy, how can we do enjoy, we know there will be big loss, if we are unable to dispatch materials today.

Director Replied: Dear Gentleman, I am an owner of this company, I select machine, I select the product, which I want to produce here, this is the time come, where, I have to use my creativity, knowledge, experience to start machine. You are having opportunity to short out but failed, so let me try.

Director and other reached at production area near machine, all employees were standing. Director start checking all perimeters. He took Screwdriver, hammer, and other required accessories. Started scrutinize the issue. There was around trying 30-minute time to resolve the problems. Finally, the machine restart. There was happiest moment, all employee and director were smiling & heartbeat goes down.

"ALL MANAGEMENT OF ORGANIZATION ATTITUDE WILL CHANGE. IT WILL GIVE HIGH EFFICIENCY, WORKABILITY AND PRODUCTIVITY IN YOUR WORK PLACE".

After restarting the machine, director said to all team. Whenever this kind of problem arise, today I solved, but next time you have to remember, how to short out. So, our productions will never stop and run long time. We are king of our mind, god has given us two eye, two hand and creative mind, just think little polite and positively, that I can solve this problem, why need hurry, we have ability to do all things because we are king of our mind. I am a king of my respective work. So, let's celebrate and concentrate on your work to make delivery by today evening.

After Saying these few motivated words, director went to his cabin.

All employees were discussing to each other's. Our director is gentleman. He didn't angry, he is so polite and decent to us. We had not taken lunch same he also not taken; he continuously noticed the issue in the productions. He was thinking that production team not taken lunch so he did not take, what a Great personality. He privileges us, he respects us. He personally is like a great man and he solve the issue, he guided (directed) us, really, he is great man and great nature. He knows his responsibility, attitude and behavior, He can easily solve the worst situation. Really, we have to salute our director.

"" WE CAN ALWAYS FOUND HAPPINESS IN DARKNEES TIME. IF, WE ARE INTERNALLY STONG TO SWITCH ON THE LIGHT"""

Remark: What we learn here, if we have any kind of situation arise, we don't have to show immediate reaction, because your immediate reaction always creates your negative impression among others. Why we have to allow other person to say wrong words about us, what director said above, we are king of our mind and expertise in our respective work.

Our attitude is our brand, which create our valued and respect of our brand image, that build images of respective personality among others, if you are running your business, to understand the heart of your business and employees are working there. Your attitude must be on such a way that other people like you and follow you.

"" WHEN YOUR WORKER OR EMPLOYEE START FOLLOWING YOU, AUTOMATICALLY YOUR BUSINESS GROWTH IS INCREASE.""

We know, that everyone is identified them self who they are? Same as in our business workplace, we have to identify our image among other employees. Sometimes people or our employees notice us, they observe that what our owner is doing.

One man has decided to open a new company as Manufacturer, He invested Rs 150 Lacs for plants and machineries, started manufacturing unit as a proprietary. He well design furnish office, staffing an employee, loaded with raw material and start productions, the company is small manufacturing unit. Everything goes well and business is running.

Owner thought, everything goes well in his business as per planning. All employees are coming and they do their allotted work very well. Sometimes, owner at factory after 10 a.m. in the morning and leave before 4 p.m. or 5 p.m. at evening. After long days, it was happening daily. The owner has received the quarterly report. He found the Productions, Sales, Purchase, recovery, graphs are decreased as compare to other quarterly reports. He noticed office staff are working Stressful. They always seen in tension. The owner thought something is going wrong, if this happen again, my business will be going down. So first he started to find what will be the reason due to my business and business environment is unbalancing.

The company have office time is morning 9 a.m. to 6 p.m., office work starts by 9.15 p.m. maximum times the employees were about late to enter in office, because they know, their owner is coming late by 10 p.m. or 10.30 p.m. But sharp 6 p.m. They were ready to leave their office, the owner was leaving office by 4.00

p.m.

Due to above, the director noticed, if the employees are late in office. Respectively around 30-minute, time is waste, also by sharp 6 p.m., they are planning to leave office because owner is not in office. Employees are planning to Complete their work 1 hour before leaving time, some time the employees have a work but make their lazy nature, Tomorrow morning. they do a pending work because to be ready to leave factory.

Why required to do today's work on tomorrow. Lingering the work for next day. The owner decided himself, that I am main reason for this situation. He thought himself. Let's change the environments, He started to join office early by 8.30 a.m.

Next day morning, owner reached office by 8.30 a.m. Some employees entered in office around by 9.30 p.m., they all noticed that boss in the office early, even at evening time, by 5 p.m. He requested all employees about the reporting their works, which they were achieved.

He started to make busy their employees, started to motive and inspire them. He tried for 1 month only, daily morning he came by 8.30 a.m. and leaving by 7.00 p.m. all employees noticed that boss is coming office earlier then us, even motivate us, report of work and many more.

All employees were noticing about the changes in the workplace and nature of their boss. They started to enter in office by sharp 9.00 am time. They start follow their boss, simultaneously, the business run in systems.

Again, Director, called meeting for quarterly progress report, he found the growth in their business, even the growth in appointed employees also.

DHARMESH GAJJAR

CHAPTER: 3

THE SKILLS REQUIRED TO BE A GREAT BUSINESSMAN

What makes sense of successful entrepreneur to build a successful organization. They have to accept certain decision. Which are some expertise knowledge and technical skill. They have to identify some special characteristics of an entrepreneurs or business owners. They have to implement some characteristics like Creativity, Communication skill, Leadership, and many more. Without this, we are not defining successful businessman.

To starting a business, or going to became an entrepreneur, it's important to develop your successful businessman skill, so that you may work or do your job accordingly with your quality skills. You have to understand the special kind of expertise skill to develop your business next level.

Sometime, I found many entrepreneurs have risk taking business. They are either success or unsuccess. Some are having their organization as a well organize, they don't want to work in their organization, but their organize employees are working for their organization.

It's an interesting question? Many entrepreneurs are thinking. How to do this? This interesting question to be solve very easy by an organize entrepreneur, because they have special kind of skills, which they implement among other employees or staffs working under the organization. Which directly effect to grow business. It will make very easy way to became a successful and develop the owner image among various industries.

Sometime, many entrepreneurs are stuck off in work, they are confused, this is only happened, when they are unaware of special skills, along with him, all respective staff (employees) are also stuck off. What they want to know and what they are doing. It will directly affect reputation of company and the owner. which decline your graph of business growth, due to this some business can't get their desired goal in selected time frame.

""IF YOU AR NOT MOVING CLOSSER TO YOUR EMPLOYEE.

YOU ARE NOT DOING ENOUGH FOR OUR BUSINESS GROWTH""

With my personal industrial experience, I defined some sort of skill that required to be successful entrepreneur or businessman. Which help you to grow yourself and your business.

➢ Effective Communications skill.
➢ Interpretation kills

CHAPTER: 4

NECESSITY OF COMMUNICATIONS

Planning to run business, it is an art and a golden opportunity, because you are selected by yourself with ideas and opportunities. Same as your employees are there in your organizations are interested to do work and grow your business. You have strong and bonding effective communications with all who are nearest you. For doing any business, this effective communication is required day to day, with whom you are dealing or working, it may be staff members, business clients, senior, junior or family, friends. Effective communications will help you to short out issue, proper reply, also it supports us to learn new and new opportunity. It is also a creative activity, how you present your work or communicate with other.

I hope, you may aware, many businesses are failing due to lake of communication skill, it is between owner and staff, worker and managers, with client, customer or suppliers, its directly effect on business, and may more aspects. To became successful business man, have to build up a brand yourself, the owner must need to implement or organize the communications skill in different way, through which its direct affect the business growth.

The organize business always offer special treatments to their employees, they communicate in such a way that, they show interest only in other needs, they try to give best possible and right answer to others. In this case others may be client customer, buyer or any one, they identify, what was your reply, if reply is in their favor, they try to listen you more, they have more interest to contact you again and again. It may be creating the image of company. Same kind of effective communications is required in your business organizations for growth.

Newly graduate student, started job in multinational company as an assistant manager export. That company was well organized, one day his senior manager told: next week I'm on 1-week holiday, going back to my home for attending family marriage function. So, all my duties and work you have to follow, I'm authorize you, so you have to take charge.

"" MANY BUSINESSES ARE FAILING DUE TO LAKE OF COMMUNICATION SKILL, IT IS BETWEEN OWNER AND STAFF, WORKER AND MANAGERS, WITH CLIENT, CUSTOMER OR SUPPLIERS""

He replied: ok no problem, will do.

The day came when he took charge of his boss, that day

one Export consignment going to Europe, it was around 17 containers.

From dispatch department, he got a telephonic call.

He picks up call, said: Hello,

Dispatch manager reply: As you aware today our export consignments are going to ready for dispatch, we have to prepare some export documents for shipping line along with invoice and other documents, we have required currency conversion rates of USD and EURO. Can you pls arrange, what are the rates today?

He replied: sure sir, I can help you out, But I need an official mail from your end, because I'm in charge of my manager work.

Dispatch manage: sure, I will.

After few minutes, he got a mail from dispatch department. He checked current rates online are USD 1.00 = 72 INR & EURO 1.00 = 83 INR. He replied the mail, and confirmed by phone call, at evening closing time 5.30 p.m. He left the company, went to his home.

By 8.30 p.m. in clock, he was taking his dinner. He got a phone call on his mobile from Dispatch manager, he picks up a call, said: Hello...

Dispatch manager replied: You have given wrong Currency rates, so we can't do factory stuffing and sealing now, tomorrow is ETD – Expected time of Departure. Booked vessels will leave, if we can't load the material. We will have big loss, today night, we have to move container to Mumbai JNPT Port. Because of giving wrong information's, we can't process today, due to your irresponsible mail, our company get big loss. (dispatch manger starts blaming him).

He replied: Cool down sir, I'm coming factory right now.

He disconnected the phone and ready to go factory, at factory in his office. He first checked the mail, what was written on mail, checked all parameter of currency rates, found he wrote all right information. He checked 2-3 times. He thought, why dispatch manager is blaming him. Immediately he went to dispatch department to meet the manager. He reached there. Started discussing with dispatch manger.

He said: Yes sir, I'm here, please check the mail, I wrote, which is right information's. show me the invoice and documents, let me check the issue.

Factory manager give him documents. He checked, he found the Currency rate was written wrong in invoice, it was written by dispatch manger or his team.

He said to dispatch manager: sir, pls check the documents, you have written, the wrong currency rates on involves, it's not my fault, it has been written by your departmental team. I am not in fault for this problem.

"" NEWLY APPOINTED EMPLOYEE PERFORMS AND COMMUNICATE WITH ALL ANGLE.

BUT A SINGLE SMALLEST ERROR FROM DISPATCH DEPARTMENTS, THAT EMPLOYEE HAVE TO LEAVE HIS JOB.""

Factory manager Replied: I am not interested to talk to you right now, will talk tomorrow morning office hour with all board members of company. You don't know, but we have big loss due to this problem. He stands up, and went without saying any words.

Next day morning, invited him to attend the board meeting, all were discussing about yesterday's consignments issue. Due to organize company policy, if the problem occurs by any employees, he/ she has to fire its compulsory. He thought he is safe, because he had some evidence of communications. During the meeting all management team were in favor of dispatch dept. Finally, the decision was taken by all board members.

The operation director said, Gentleman, we are fire you, if you have a filed bond, we will ruin it. Listing this word, he was shock,

He put his question: Can I suppose to know the specific reason to fire me and ruin my bond.

The Operation Director Reply: We know whose fault; we just obey the policies of our organization. We required experience person as you are newly appointed, you will get other jobs soonest, but dispatch manager will not, also we want to use their expertise skill also.

With fascinating answer, he didn't have any words to defense, he went to his cabin,

From above, we can easily identify the small mistake became a big issue, a big problem. Newly appointed employee performs and communicate with all angle. But a single smallest error from dispatch departments, that employee have to leave his job. The fault was dispatch departments. They not recheck the currency rate, even they wrote in documents, none of the dispatch departments staff checked the documents. This was happening because of lake of Communications skill among the departmental staffs. Many businesses are there, they are facing some hectic problem because of gap in communication.

CHAPTER: 5

WHY INTERPRETATION FOR YOUR BUSINESS?

If, I would like to sell Parle biscuit of Rs 5.00 /-, you can take it and pay me Rs 5.00 /-. Now I change, if I give you empty packet (removing all biscuits). Can you take this? will you pay me Rs 5.00 /-. I know the answer, it's obviously NO. now the question is, if I give you biscuit with and without packing of worth Rs 5.00 /- now think in details whose value? Biscuit or without biscuit. You can be creative and pressure on your mind. The answer will arise, value is Brand Parle and value is Biscuit. Right.

But you are wrong, there is no value of brand Parle and biscuits. You may be confused, and agar to know, whose value, if not brand and biscuits.

Let's go some other way, we know some biggest

personality people write some name of their home name plate, if you are passing nearest to that home. What will you think, if you want to go his home? Why someone asks some information's, then we will guide them to meet someone.

He may guide you well. Why you are excited to meet them, u don't know him and home. Pressure on your mind, it's interesting. You may think, this home is good, let's go, you may think the owner is good, let's go. Here same as Parle biscuits, the nameplate outside of home is Brand, and the people in the home are very good it's a product (like biscuit). Now pressure on your mind, which one have valued, people in home or name plate of home.

I know, you may me confused, what author want to elucubrate. Well, let's come to point of view. When I ask this type of question in many corporate training seasons, most of the people replied the valued is products, but they don't pay me Rs 5.00 because there is no biscuit, at that time I say, if you not purchase the empty packing because of not having biscuits inside, you clearly mention the valued is products not brand.

"" THE BUSINESS OWNER OR AN ENTREPRENEUR MUST BE INSPIRED AND COLLECT MAXIMUM INFORMATION TO IMPLEMENT IN THEIR BUSINESS WORKPLACE""

Now be clear, there is no value of brand. Someone replied opposite, the valued is brand written on packing, so we purchase branded material. The valued is brand. But they are not purchasing empty packing. Accordingly, them, valued is brand not products.

Again, be clear, the value is a brand, not products. Be emphasis on this subject. If there is no valued of brand and material, then who's valued?

Why would I like to visit your home, because the people in your home are decent and kind toward the guest, who visit their home. They give their best possible services to every visitor. It means the people, who are living in home are most important valued person, who keep their services consistency among other visitors. Every visitor thinks, very good home, nice people, all are organized, never disappoint anyone. Good kind of hospitality. And many more.

Compare this with the Parle biscuits package, you like to purchase because you know the biscuits is a product, which is very good, testy, every time you found the same quality test. Due to this quality test of biscuits, that you people know the Parle brand biscuits. But who make a consistency quality of biscuits, it is made by the employees or worker who are working in Parle biscuit organization?

Same as a home, the people of home are giving their best servicing, so you want to visit that home again, same here in any industries like Parle, the employees or worker are doing their best job and give consistency quality products, then the value is the employees of the organization.. they are maintaining the consistency products and your business image grow up. The brand gets famous. Accordingly, your business brand, the image of the owner of the companies also develop.

"" EVERY EMPLOYEE OF THE ALL DEPARTMENTS ARE CREATIVE, SUPPORTIVE AND MOTIVATE""

Your business is organized, the owner has to develop the interpretation skill among the employee and workers. Always gives inspiration to their employees, the interpretation skill is very essential part, through which your organization brand image became your individual brand image.

We have lots of things nearest, we get inspiration from them. The business owner or an entrepreneur must be inspired and collect maximum information to implement in their business workplace. We don't imagine, that, there are two electric switches in our room. These two switches are doing their work, if I push switch 1, the light is on, and again push, the light gets off. Same I do for switch 2, it performs same as switch 1.

Keep in mind the role of both switches. Now imaging the role of your two employees in same departments, now compare both work employees and switches. From the desk of owner or manager the instructions are giving to their staff, they have to perform accordingly instructions same as a switch, switch-1 is performing, switch-2 is not reacting, simultaneously switch-2 is working. Switch-1 is not reacting. Both are doing their job, if switch-1 is off, means your one staff member is on leave, then we can joint the electric wires -with switch-2. And push it, both lights are on, the switch-2 is not reacting that I will not do. I will not send single to switch-1 light. Same as one employee on leave, other have to instruct so he can take charge and do both work simultaneously. they need to understand each other.

The owner of any organizations has to keep in their mind, to run business and develop brand, they have to design the workplace with such type of understandable, supportable, interpretation skill. This is more helpful for any business to grow up and create a brand.

Entrepreneur have to design the environment in such way, that every employee of the all departments are creative, supportive and motivate. If the employees have their internal issue, that will be most dangerous factor, owner is responsible for this. So, they have to design a workplace model with this kind of special skills.

"THE QUEALITY OF YOUR THINKING
IS
THE QUALITY OF THE BUSINESS YOU ARE DOING.

Be countable thinking of an owner, which acts major role for business environment, there will be quality in you, you will deserve yourself as quality personality. Running a business with quality of thinking, the entire staff of your workplace will update with your quality thinking. That will be most useful tool for doing work. growing business and create the responsible brand.

CHAPTER: 6

HOW YOUR EMPLOYEE CREATE BRAND?

in year 2015, I was on Europe Business Trip, City Prague, Chezh republic. I was staying in one of 5-star hotel, I was stayed 4 night. As we know Europe countries are mostly non vegetarian. I am an Indian and vegetarian, I don't like non veg food.

1st day in morning breakfast time, I went to restaurant, the lady manager, age around 50 - 55 years was watching towards me, that I am taking Milk and Fruits for breakfast. (She Observed me)

2nd day morning same time, I want for Breakfast in the restaurant. First, I see all available foods on counter, I took dish with Fruits and Milk, then sat on my table.

Something happens, that lady manager was watching me and noticed that this Indian person is not taking any foods on breakfast time.

She came to my table and asked me a question, Are you Vegetarian?

I replied: yes, I'm vegetarian.

She just talked and went away.

3rd day in morning same time, I went for Breakfast, same as yesterday, I took dish with Fruits and Milk, and sat on my table.

Same thing happens, that lady manager was watching me and noticed that this Indian person is not taking any food on breakfast time.

She came to my table and asked me: why don't you not try for some egg's items like Omelets, half fry?

I replied: I am a vegetarian and don't eat Egg also. I like to eat only veg.

I also added more words: Many items are non veg, made with meat, chicken and eggs. I don't prefer to eat this kind of foods, because of vegetarian.

She said: I understand, but as a restaurant manager, I really don't like, any of our hotel guest don't take breakfast.

I said: that's great and it's your duty and your satisfactions.

She was disappointed and said, I saw you are one more day here, (tomorrow is your last day). So, tomorrow morning when will you are here for breakfast, please meet me first than take your breakfast.

I replied: ok I will inform you.

4th day was my last day. And I have to check out by 11.00 a.m. because of having return flight on 4 p.m.

In the morning, I entered in to restaurant, that lady manager was at counter talking with her other staff members.

I thought, why have to contact her, as I'm in hurry to check out, have to pack my luggage and all. so, I took dish with some fruits and milk, finally sat on one of empty table.

Just took a 2 pcs of fruit pcs, she looked toward me, she sent one lady waiter to pick up my dish. That lady waiter came and pick up my dishes.

I replied: what are you doing? I didn't complete my breakfast.

She replied immediately: Sir, you are our valuable guest, please wait, we are preparing a special dish for you.

I was sitting there for 10-15 minute, only drinking Milk. One of lady waiter came and serve me an Italian Pizza- it was around 1.5 feet size. With some souse and pickles.

That was the greatest day, because since last 4 days I didn't eat proper food, I got pizza and I eat. When I completed my pizza. That lady waiter came and serve me an Indian Masala Dosa. That was also very testy and I enjoyed.

Again, she came with Onion Uthappa, my stomach was already full but the test was awesome and I enjoy all three dishes.

During eating last item Onion Uthappa, that Lady Manager came and sat on my table.

She starts saying: Hello sir, did you enjoy this special Indian food.

I replied, yes mam, I really enjoy and happy, that after very long time, I eat this kind of dish giving satisfaction to my stomach and body.

We have had some more discussion going on, but one question was in my mind, which I asked her: why you prepare a special dish for me? any specific reason.

She replied very politely: Sir, you are our guest, and guest is our god, as a restaurant manager, my duty is to look after all guests. When, I was noticing you that you didn't take breakfast, I felt unhappy by my heart. So, I decided to do something for you.

I said: I understand, as an employee of organizations, customer satisfaction is required. But I personally didn't demand for any kind of such food. But let me know how did you make this?

She smiles little and replied: since last 2 days, I understood that you are Indian and vegetarian, so I decide to searv Indian famous dish. To be frank, yesterday evening, when I was at my home. I studied some Indian recipe of Dosa, Pizza & Uthappa on internet, I tried at my home, I served to my Husband and children. I was very much happy to share this that my husband and children, they liked this test awesome. They enjoyed lots of.

I was watching her face; she was very happy and her face was glow with smile and all.

She also added, Sir, you don't know but I say, today these three-item you eat, was not prepared by a cook available here, it is prepared by myself. I was inside the kitchen and I personally prepared this.

I was shocked and fascinated with this answer, & replied, you cook this, you are the manager of this restaurant. It's interesting. I can't stop my words and asked the simple question.

Why you cook?

She was very gentle lady, replied on those way, and I believe what the importance of Customer Satisfaction in any kind of business.

""" UNTIL UNLESS YOU ARE NOT SATISFIED YOUR CUSTOMERS OR CLIENTS, THEY WILL NOT JOIN YOU AGAIN""

Her replied was: Sir, I am an employee of this 5-start hotel, hotel give me salary for my duties. My duties are giving best services all guests who are staying here. You are one of them. Everyone want their value of their invested money; I am also having the valued salary, that, I received from this hotel. You are a guest of this hotel, you didn't take breakfast, you keep your stomach empty. Which makes me unhappy.

I decided, how to make happy my client, spent maximum time, search maximum on internet. Tried at my home, make my family happy, served and tested to my family and I try for you.

Today I'm sitting and talking with you, I know you are very much happy, and satisfied your stomach. Customer is our god, I want, when will be you come again Prague, you will book this hotel, not other. To make good brand image of our hotel, I am employee, giving better and the best services to our guest, so guest will be come again, it directly the % of booking are increases and growth of our hotels.

I said her, Today I'm leaving your hotel as well as this country also, but any of my Colleagues, friends and family member visit Prague, I will recommend your hotel name for booking and stay here.

Remark: This is Mr. Gajjar's Personal Experience during Prague visit. He said any kind of biggest industries or hotel you have. Until unless you are not satisfied your customers or clients, they will not join you again. It directly effects on brand image. But if you can satisfy your clients, they will rejoin you, which increase your maximum sales, you can get maximum return of Invest money on marketing.

Mr. Gajjar said – First understand what your client or customer need, (same as Lady Manager- She understand that Mr. Gajjar is Indian and eat only veg). You can offer them what they want. If client get satisfactory from your end. They will book you till the time they need your services. Which will increase your image and business. Keep relation and give your best services, so the client can't go with other suppliers, they will do business with your lifetime.

CHAPTER: 7

NEED TO ORGANIZE YOU AND

YOUR BUSINESS

When we are planning to start up new organization or you are running your business, the most important factor is to organize your business. Before organizing the business, you as an owner must have to organize yourself. Your self-evolution is most important to design or organize your business.

To organize the business. You have to self-evaluations yourself with internal effort and responsibilities. You must have to care other, short out the situations with best possible ways, that deliver your excellent personalities. You must have the motivating and convincing power among others and technique of communications and self-confidence leadership building.

"" SUCCESS IS A SCIENCE, IF YOU HAVE THE CONDITION, YOU WILL DEFINETLY GET RESULT.""

We know we have very busy hectic life, having a stuck off of daily activities. Sometime, we pay attention on our work or not? Sometime, we feel uncomfortable to do work because of hectic life mental stress. We like to stay alone and ignore others. This is also happening in our family, friends and in business. Due to this, sometime our relations, image and prestige have negative effect among others. Same thing happens on your business also. We can't think, it is easy to solve, its big issue to short out for better growth.

We know, all above and can be settle the stuck off life, it is only possible when you organize yourself and organize your business. Many businesses have their organize staff, worker even required machineries and articles to work on proper manner to eliminate the stressful work environments.

We know, some have poor organizations have poor output like maximum waste of time and money, and some have organized organization, have maximum saving time and money. In your organization, you have to add some effort to organize your organization. If above characteristics, you have, it means you are SMART and organize: S- Specific, M- Measurable, A- Attitude, R-respectable, T- Time Management.

One day one business owner got ready to go office. Before leaving his home, he was standing front of mirror. While watching his face in the mirror, he starts asking himself, who are you? which angle you looks like a great businessman? Do you spend valued time in the office? Is everything going systematically as pe your ideas and plan?

He was reading his face and body language. He thought let's change and started to evaluate himself, to build my name, image and personality, I'm not perfect now. I have to organize myself in way that, I can say loudly, that I will be tension free. He went to office, & Start changing himself, with his body language, reaching office on time, start given 100 % concentration on work. Started to take care and motivate his staff, clients, customer and suppliers. Within 1 month he got a positive result in him and in business organisation. He found the changes and growth.

"" SELF MOTIVATKOINS IS ONLY A SIMPLE WAY

THAT FORCE YOU TO CHANGE"""

We know, owner is responsible person for their business, because any problem, any loss or profit or any kind of situation, he has to tackle. To handle these all situations, required himself to be evaluate properly. They have to decide under which organize categories; they are looking. Like Organize people, un organize people, or pseudo type organize people.

The organize people category is belong to 100% Percent Organize them self, who wear proper cloth, keep himself free, systematic time being and many more characteristics. They make their nature, such a way that, they look different than others. To learn more about these kinds of organize people, I decided to meet some people.

I called a person: Hello Sir, I would like to meet you, can you give me an appointment.

He replied: yes sure, but pls wait a few minutes, let me check my diary, will tell you time and date. After 2 minutes, he spoke, today is Monday, you may come to visit me on Wednesday by 4.00.p.m. Sharp, I will give you 30 minutes only, because of having another meeting by 4.30 p.m.

I replied: Thank you very much for giving an appointment, I will be there on time.

On Wednesday, I went to his office, I park my car outside his business premises. The Gate keeper (security) opened the door, he smiled and respectfully said, you are Mr. Gajjar, you have a meeting with our company's Owner, please give me your visiting card, we will make your entry. I was shocked, that security officer said his assistant, go with sir and show him the office of our owner.

"" THE ORGANIZE PEOPLE CATEGORY IS BELONG TO 100% PERCENT ORGANIZE THEM SELF.

WHO WEAR PROPER CLOTH, KEEP HIMSELF FREE, SYSTEMATIC TIME BEING AND MANY MORE CHARACTERISTICS.""

He came and guide me. When I was entering in the office, found all are neat and clean, peoples (staff) were working, there were no noise, looks like silence and decent atmosphere.

I knock the door, slightly open the gate of owner cabin and said, May I coming Sir? that owner himself stand up from his chair, came toward the door and handshake me and said Pls come, I'm waiting for you.

He handshake me by right hand and he put his left hand on my beck side of shoulder. I notice his body language, Even I also notice his cloth were perfect as business man, his table was neat and clean, only laptop and diary were on the table. I was fascinated after watching and noticing this all.

I have started on discussing on the subject for that the meeting was arranged. He was listing very politely and decent way, he replied his answer point to point only. In 15-minutes, our meeting was over, in 15-minute duration time, his peon came and serve me water, tea and biscuits. During the meeting, I asked him a one question: Sir, I am really shock, fascinated that your office is different than other, everything is on their place, even during the meeting, you handover your phone to your assistant, so our meeting is not disturbing. Really it surprising me.

""BE CLEAR IN YOUR MIND. TO KNOW WHO IS WRONG? AND WHAT IS WRONG? THIS WILL KEEP OUR STRONG RELATIONS.""

He replied with his value: Gentleman, Mr. Gajjar, I personally organize myself, and organize my workplace. I know who am I? and would like to be life time. Which is creating a positive image among other and our staff members. You can see this wall, here we posted every month sales growth details. You can easily read, every month our sales are increased by 5 % Percentage. now u can image, systematic growth in our business, because of this organize environments and organized nature.

He added more, when I'm going to visit any other organization, they are un organize, or pseudo organize, Something when we are talking, they are in hurry to reply, all material are over his table, they don't take breakfast, lunch and dinner property, always show busy himself. In this type of situation, we can't give attention in our work or business. it has a direct impact on our business, office staff, and family also, our business can't grow up, it fluctuates ups and down, problem with quality, material, systems, and many more.

This unorganized people and business set up, don't have their proper goal and plan, they just think and do, but in hurry, without thinking and organizing himself.

I also added some words from my end. Last week, I met one person of age 40, Same like you a 30-minute talk. When I was entering his office, all staff member are cleaning their table and re-put the thing on their place, I asked that person, Sir, What are your employees dong now, is any special occasions is coming.

He said, noting, a foreign delegate is coming tomorrow. So, we are doing this, he can understand that we are same like them. What we are, we are happy, but to show different to foreign delegate.

I thought myself this type of person are pseudo organize type, they just want to show unreal thing to other, these types of peoples are only trying to pretend to be organize, they are trying to convince other that he is great, educated mind, but actually he did not. This type of personalities is passing fake information. Something they irritating other, they can't understand what they want to elucubrate.

It was really an amazing experience to meet with a organize people. Then I left his office.

CHAPTER: 8

ORGANIZE YOUR BUSINESS AS A BRAND.

To organizing your business is very simple ways, it's just a managerial part to decide the ways of organizing organizations, it depend upon the company structure. There is not required to implementing any kind of technologies.

The owner and his managerial team have to systemize accordingly their particular industries requirements. You have to look at the picture of your organization, where you want to see it in couple of years.

If your company unorganized, so you can focus on small

part of areas. But when your entire business organization is well organized, you may focus on big area for developing, designing, upgradations and expansions.

You, as an owner must have at your business organizations, you have to notice yourself that your business is running as per your vision and mission, this thought will determine you, that your business is organize or not organize. Be practical in this point. Because your designed vision and mission will give your profitable business, if it's not, the business can't run profitable.

There will be big issue you may face. Customer, supplier will notice you, more than your products. If the same thing is organizing as pe mission and vision, one day your business organizations will be in listed in top most companies list.

"" TRY TO ENJOY TO BECAME A STRONG, WHEN ALL WORLS ARE TRYING TO WEEK YOU.""

To organize your business required some important factor is the vision and mission of your organizations, where exactly you want to see your company, Design the goal for your organizations, it may be short or long, Tray to Achieve short goal first, every achieved short goal will allow to achieve a big goal. You need to design a plan accordingly your goal set, the plan will be systematic like goal, short term or long term, you and your entire business organizations team must have to follow accordingly the design plan.

If you have design your goal and plan, which your employees does not know, it will be big challenging, because they don't know goal of each departments, for this you must have to aware your employees about it, guide them, motivate them, accordingly they can perform their respective role for better profitability business.

An organization employee must understand the specific goal of organizations. Here you have to be open with your employee's workplace, need to motivate them, train them, share your guidance how to achieve goal, there will be motivations required every aspect of business environment for and employees. Due to this, employees understand you and organizations so they put their ideas and creativities to make workplace more effective and productive.

You may aware that, to organize the staff is most critical and challenging job. the biggest issue in any kind of business organizations is interpretation and communications skills. It means the work does not float effectively from one department to another department. You as an owner have to think about this situation, because it directly effects on your environment of business, it is creating the Slow process

If you are in to planning to start business, you have to create plan accordingly design your business. Once plan is created, remain part is to organize the nature of an organization.

You have to design or organize the assign work departments wise, have to assign the task, works or duties of various department of an organization. Due to this all manager of their departments are coordinate with their teams, employees, worker even the people outside of business who are directly or indirectly connected with your organization. All managerial team have to understand the Company plan, goal, also all managerial team must aware about the lows policies of an organization.

One company get big order, they have planned for production & Purchase, they place raw material orders to their supplier, them of one order is import. Company pay advance for import orders, they started producing product 24 hours. Everyday productions are going routine, the raw material stock getting empty, they required the imported material as soon as possible. Producing team inform to purchase department, we are in highly demand the imported material.

if we will not receive in coming few days, we have to stop production. That was the challenging time for that company. The purchasing team regularly follow up with shipping company about the status of container.

A Company placed Import order, last day the imported material stocks getting empty, on the morning a call received form Shipping agent to purchase departments. Sir, your import shipments is arrived at Mumbai JNPT port. We need some documents for custom clearance, I am going to send an email with check list of documents, please resend immediate with requested documents. So today, once we received, will do custom clearance and release the cargo to send for delivery at your factory. Purchase Import manager replied, ok pls do accordingly, we will respond.

Within 15 minutes, they received mail from Shipping agent. The company has designed a system, any mail receives on server, within 30 minutes, they have to respond. Respective purchase team send relevant documents to Freight forwarding agent. The container released from custom clearance, later in evening, they have received the material at their factory. Next day when the productions get stop, that can't stop because of raw material is now in stocks.

We can note easily, this company is organizing himself with all managerial team, what we have to do focus and how to do, to complete production of big orders, all departments design a plan and set a goal to complete order in selected time frame.

His company is fully organizing by people, by software, by communications, and other point of view, due to this they don't face any kind of pressure from other departments, no mental stress, all things are going smoothly. Any organize organizations gives their first priority to focus only in doing important things.

While staff is organized, all employees and staff have to focused on what is important to work to first. Remind yourself of your long-term goals and remind to your employees when necessary. Set daily priorities to meet your goals.

Sometime when we get phone call, we said, I can't talk to you now, can you call next Monday by 11 a.m. when the next Monday cam, they call you by 11 a.m. sharp. It's really intersecting, 1 week before given time for call, that man call him on given time. This is only happening when; we note in our diary or make list for call.

Some company have some systems when they leave office by evening, they have to completed that day task, they have to write checklist of doing important tasks on tomorrow, not todays pending. Giving daily priority to do complete the day work. Sometime the owner has priority to do their job. They also make such kind of check list for themselves. This will count the image of company, because of organizing things creates the brand image of yours and your company itself.

CHAPTER: 9

BRAND IMAGE OF AN ORGANIZE BUSINESSMAN.

There are lot of people on the universe are doing their own business, it may be small, medium or large-scale business, they have their all defined character and personality to run their business, when we are thinking about some successful business man, they already failure then became a success. It is because of their special kind of strategic characteristics.

This businessman has some special dynamic enthusiastic and positive looks, they are always driven nature, they look to drive their business grow, I always found many businessmen they only talk and plan to develop their business next level.

They know when they start it was ground level, always do target up from their level, if you are successful businessman or going to be, then you must have such characterizes to drive your business up next stage. Successful businessman always does challenging work, so they became a motivation himself and other who surround him. They are always mentor and have good determination power.

In our life, during the study in collage or universities, we make a plan or design a goal to Crack the exams, or to achieve some level in education, we give our best performance because we have a specific targeted goal. Its take time to struggle but at the end, we get. We learn lots of and get wide experience.

Same you are business man To make your business is your brand, then you must be a goal oriented. You have specific targeted goal, vision, mission. Most of success business run by successful businessman because they design their goal with vision. they take more time to set a goal, with clear objective they get the result.

Many businessman or entrepreneur are failure to run business, but their most confident in their work, they have powerful enthusiasm leadership action. In any situation, any time, they can handle the situation and run business. This kind of confident people never seen negative, always do work positive and energetic, even they can lead the team with full of enthusiasm and courage. Confident businessman always ready to take decision, they never stop in their work. They just focus to work done, so they became more success in their life. But those businessmen, who are lazy, less confident or dependable their business is steady, can't became a successful.

I found many times; some people have some kind of

passion in their life. It may be driving, work, or any special areas. If they got such passion, they became passionate to do work by heard, they invest their maximum time, enjoy and involve till happy. I have seen this kind of passionate nature in business man or entrepreneur also, they have a special characteristic like passion, they are very excited and involve in their work every day. They enjoy their work, also pay higher attention and concentration. This passionate nature business man are successful businessman or entrepreneurs.

Mr. Patel is the Owner of X company call to Mr. Mehta owner of Y company. Mr. Patel requested Mr. Mehta to purchase our Product (raw material) of Rs 110 P kg. Mr. Patel's job is to do marketing and selling his products, Mr. Mehta's job is purchase and negotiation.

Mr. Mehta replied, Mr. Patel, according to received indent from production. I'm in need of your material, to be frank we are running with some sort of funds, we have limitation of funds. We want to buy your material because its technically suitable for our products.

Due to some funding issue, we can't pay Rs 110 p kgs, we want to book this order by Rs 98 p kgs. Hope you can do it for us. Mr. Patel Replied, I understand about your finance issue, we are also having some sort of funds. We will be agreed to supply you of Rs 98 p kgs, but you have to pay 100 % advance and quantity 15000 kgs in one lot. I will give you special discount and big volume of material. Hope you can agree.

Above paragraph, it's been clear. Both are successful businessman, they have their ideas to business and grove business, Mr. Mehta is somehow budget minded businessman, they want to run business with negotiation in price, so he can down his manufacturing cost. Mr. Patel is also successful business man with strategic convincing power.

He can give negotiable price, but he put condition to offer targeted price if Mr. Mehta give 100 % advance and bulk quantity orders. Both businessman characteristics are money minded, one interested to reduce the productions cost & other want money in advance with discounted price. Entrepreneur of businessman must be budget minded and strategic decision maker. They can save maximum money in business to grow business.

My favorite characteristics for specially those business man or entrepreneurs, who have small or medium business, owner is independent, they can take any decision himself without intimating other departments, he did not need to ask anyone's suggestion or input. He himself king of his mind, and self-reliance. These self-reliant characteristics is an important role for taking any decision to grow their business. There may be possibilities to became a successful businessman.

Along with self-reliance, some businessmen are humble by nature. They are looking some suggestions form their respective managements teams. Some entrepreneur doesn't want credit on him, they give credit to their team who gives suggestion. Due to this they make their good image among employees or management. Owner must be open minded, they must be open with their managements or employees,

Whenever we are confused to get some ideas or suggestion, we open our mind, and trying to share with some expert people or other alternative like family, friend, relative. Due to openly talking, some suggestion or output we received from others. That is somehow some innovating or new one. Which help us to think different or perform. Same way, you do your business, successful business man are open minded, they always try to capture information's and ideas from other, they implement those in their business strategies, which makes them successful businessman.

CHAPTER:
10

EMPLOYEE ARE AN ASSETS

To run any business or start up any business, the owner required some employees for different work. These employees are taking important role for an organization, which lead and key factor for the successful business. A part of doing hard work for success, employees need satisfaction form the business organization. The success of business owner and his business is only possible, when the employees of the organization are satisfied, their satisfaction directly or indirectly effect on your business customer or buyers' satisfaction. Its work wise versa.

Sometime employees are failed to satisfy their customer or

client, because they are internally not satisfied by the business organization or by owner. To grow business successfully, an organization have to pay attention to their customer or buyer satisfaction, it is only depending when your employees are happy with their organizations.

The business owners have a dream to grow their business. They must aware the main key factor is their employees, they have to keep their employees motivated for better workability and profitability, they have to maintain the employees self-confident and enthusiasm to think like entrepreneur. They have to show the business image and goals of an organization.

If the employees start think like owner, your business start grow because employees will give their dedication in work, they use their maximum effort, focus on job because they are satisfied by the organizations. To support your employees are the best remedy to grow your business.

"TAKING CARE OF YOUR EMPLOYEES, EMPLOYEES WILL TAKE CARE OF YOUR BUSINESS "

The owner part is to decide to design and set business environments. To keep happy and satisfied their employees in workplace. The owner must have to build up the employee's ownership organization. Providing regular training for motivate, confident and many more areas, which boost employees forced in their work.

One employee has master degree, recently join in marketing department. He was doing hard work, giving his maximum time in work, he leads his team, regularly doing reporting to senior and follow up with junior. One day the owner called a meeting, he checked all employees record, this employee has good track record during his work. He managements team and owner decided to give some compensation. They said we are running our business, we have to be transparent with our employees, if anyone is doing good job.

"DON'T TAKE TENTION, WHEN OTHER NOT UNDERSTAND YOU.

BECAUSE GOOD BOOKS NEVER UNDERSTAND BY EVERYONE.""

we have to appreciate them among others. The employee must satisfy that he/ her receives appreciation because of the work he is doing for the company. This will create an image of your business. If you are transparent with your employees, that how is you make your business and how to satisfy them. There will be a good working environment to success your business.

Sometime you don't expect your staff will be committed to work as entrepreneur, for your business as you are doing as an entrepreneur. There are so many complaints from various businessowners that they have labor and staff issue. They don't do hard work; they don't follow the importance of business. What can we do resolve this issue? To sort out this kind of staffing issue in organization, the owner must have to take some steps for their employees.

A company is well organized, they have to hire an employee, they publish the add in newspaper, arrange an interview. organized companies' owner is also organized, they have designed some system tool for select employees for not generating staffing issue. The interview starts. Owner Read the Biodata of candidate, he starts asking all information beside the job requirements. After few minutes the business owner put this biodata beside the table.

"WE ARE ALWAYS FIND HAPPINESS IN DARKNESS TIME.

IF WE ARE INTERNALLY STRONG TO SWITCH ON LIGHTS.""

He asked to candidate, tell me who much salary you want?

Candidate said I need USD 500 per month. 6 days week and 8 hr to work.

Business owner said, ok done, we will give. In which area you are expertise, most happy, more knowledgeable and excited a to work.

Candidate say, my best preferences is Purchase and material management.

Business owner said, congratulations dear, your jobs is done, you are hired, but have a one conditions.

Candidate said, what sir?

Owner replied: We hired as per your condition. You want your choice salary, we agree to pay, you want your choice of (interest) work, we give you, we agree your terms, now time for our terms. You have to be work with passion, motivation, energetic and goal setting, you must be leader to your allotted work, there will be not complain from your end, if the company found your activities which directly or indirectly effect on company, we will not ask you the reason why you are fire?

Here the organized business owner, interested to hire a candidate with his choice of interest and satisfactions of salary, if the owner is accepting the candidate interest, simultaneously the candidate must have to accept the company's interest. If both are simultaneously each other, companies work environment will be bright and growth oriented.

When the business is form, the owner of the company is design goal and strategic plan. Accordingly, to plan and targeted goal, the owner is looking forward to achieve in particular time frame. The employees are appointed to do work for achieve a company's goals. The role of owner is to set or allow employees to set their own goals. The owner is transparent with employee, owner give freedom to employees to set their goals.

"SYSTEMATIC PLANNING OF WORKS, ALWAYS GIVES BETTER AND BEST RESULT OUTPUT"

An organize company have specific goal and vision for their company, they always look their company is growing and interested to grow, they are planning accordingly the goal, in above para, when you hire employees and allot a work is quite difficult, the owner have selected the employees who is expertise in his work, he do work with passion and use their energy to work hard.

The owner to ask their employees about to set their goal, they make some prototype graphs and check list as well planner for doing work for employees, they intimate the employees to plan your work, set your goal, accordingly your knowledge and expertise. That will help employees to work accordingly, as we know, systematic planning, always gives better result.

After masters, In my first job was marketing, my manager encourage to set my own goal, he trusted me that I can do work, he insisted me to design a goal, he said, your target was to get order of USD 1 million in 1st quarter, and every quarter your sales growth will be increased by 5-10 %. Accordingly, I designed step by step targets, I use my knowledge, expertise and courage to write the goal, he motivated me to do work. I write my goal. I was employees there; company insist me to set my goal for grow my business.

Accordingly designed plan, first quarter, I reach the targeted goal, all management team and director of companies were happy and share best wishes. There are more 3 quarter remain, next day, I started work on my goal, every quarter I completed my goal with increased goal 5-10%. At the end of the last quarter, the growth of sales is increased by 30 %.

All management team and owner of company give me prestige and awards as best performance to grow company by 30 % Growth. This is only happening when the company give me an opportunity to set goal, design a plan, company not set a goal, goal was set by an employee who are expertise to do.

Some business organization have skill and experienced employees, they gained new skills and up level their competencies, they will be more ready to tackle the challenges within your organization. And when you proactively help employees gain new skills, not only will they become better leaders, they'll also be more loyal to your organization. These skilled experience employees are more helpful for organizations growth.

"SOMETIMES, WE SUCCESS OR UNSUCCESS.

IT DOES NOT MEAN; OUR GAME IS OVER.

SO BE POSITIVE AND GO AHEAD.""""

A company had a large number of employees, few are new and old, the old are experienced. The company gave an assignment (targeted goal) to their newly appointed employees or ground staff of employees. They are doing their work, the work is not completed in time, it takes many more times, in this situation.

if you have skill experience employees, they can guide them to work in positive direction, because they have company developing experience with vision for learning, monitoring, leading and supporting. They do train and guiding to their respective staff. With the help of skill employee's potential, the stretched assignment will be completed.

Any business organization are looking to grow, the owner must necessarily require a skill and experience personality in their managerial staff, which are always there to support in any worst situation.

Every business organization design different types of system to encourage their employees. Some organizations are looking to grow their business with to understand the feedback of their employees work & Companies products, delivery, quality and many more.

Company intimate to their marketing and purchase team, to send a feedback form to your all your client who are there in your list. Ask them fill up the feedback and return bcck to us. That feedback form is for company and for the employees who are dealing with their respective clients.

When all forms are received, the owner and the management team will scrutinize & study, this report of the company & employees are defining the business model. How is the company? and how is the services, and employees of organization. This report is also designing the how your employee's performance with their client or customers. This is also allowed company to improve and innovation for doing their work for growth.

The organized business has their employees' feedback are good, company encourage them with some compensation and awards. Which create employee's prestige, as well as employees are more interested to work hard and keep his work more specific goal oriented. Business owner have to focus on their employees for growing business.

The organize companies' managerial staff or an owner must be specific that any matter there in organization, they have to pay close attention toward the employees, how to talk, manner, words, even subjects, there must be some communications and interpretation skill is required to handle the matter. In any situation matter, the owner has to cool with positive mind, they have to guide, teach or treat positively to employees.

You are the owner or the organize company always treated their employees by saying "good job" after a project done, they highlight all what they made on a project. But you have to be specific, what you say and doing, when your employees need your support or guidelines.

Business owner have to spend time behind their employees, you will be expertise to develop courage, motivate, be specific, and   leadership in your employees. Your employees became more productive, effective, trained to handle or tackle the situation. You have to pass on their image as a good employee, giving value this will build-up their mind set for to work faster than owner.

ABOUT THE AUTHOR

Author, Mr. Dharmesh Gajjar, born in 1st March 1981, in India, state of Gujarat, He completed his Engineering, and Masters in Foreign Trade, Having Duel qualification, since 2008, he is an Entrepreneur for his manufacturing business in Gujarat.

Along with Entrepreneur, Businessman, he is also corporate trainer, soft skill trainer, mainly providing corporate training in various subjects in entrepreneurs, entrepreneurship and business development, sales, marketing, negotiation and many more,

He visited more than 15 countries, since 2008, he is getting experience and learning from various industries, since 2014, practicing as corporate trainer and business coach.

This boom is written and dedicate to those people who are going to be start business, interested to build their carrier as a successful businessman.

I hope, you will enjoy reading this book, and looking forward more new books from our side.

Thanking You

Dharmesh Gajjar